dear self,

author's note:

these words came to me over many sleepless nights and draining days of feeling unworthy, unloved and undeserving. i have turned my heart inside out time and time again to make others feel loved, but failed to return that love back into myself. this is me finally doing just that.

these words got me through my darkest of days when giving up seemed like the best option, and i hope they do the same for you. just remember that you are enough, you are loved deeply and you are everything that you need, always.

with love,
patience tamarra

for mady.
everything i do is for you.
i love you.

dear self,

you are deserving
and worthy of love.

and love is worthy
and deserving of *you*.

the love that lives in you
can cure the most
aching heart

including your own.

dear self,

you are loved
and protected.

always.

patience tamarra

you are allowed
to *grow*
at your own pace.

dear self,

within your body lies
all that you need and desire.

there is no need to seek it
elsewhere.

today give yourself
the space to feel
your emotions
without judgement.

dear self,

when the dust settles
you'll *thank god*
for the storm.

embrace *every part*
of you that they
forgot to.

dear self,

there is a
heaven
in you
waiting to be
witnessed.

open your heart.

it deserves to feel
love again.

dear self,

it is safe for you
to be your
authentic self.

you are allowed
to feel *joy*

even when others
do not.

dear self,

you can receive new love
even if you haven't
completely healed from

old wounds.

hold your heart

and say

"i love you".

dear self,

you convince yourself
you've failed
before even trying.

stop doing that.

if the dream wasn't
meant for you
the universe would've
never planted it in you
to *bloom.*

dear self,

your heart never
belonged to *them*.

your body is your
sacred temple.

it deserves all of
your worship.

dear self,

you no longer have to
rest in the pain.

you're allowed to
move on.

the threads that tie
you to your trauma are
burning away
with *flames* of joy.

bask in the celebration.

dear self,

you are allowed
to show up
fully — **without**

apology.

hold onto the lesson
not the person.

dear self,

you are whole and complete.
there is no need to
pretend to be something

you already are.

reminder —

self-love is also telling
yourself that you deserve
better from you.

dear self,

you will fall short
at times

and that's okay.

your softness
does not strip you
of your *strength.*

dear self,

pour into yourself
before you pour
into others.

even if that means
your cup
overflows.

forgive those that
made you feel
worthless.

they couldn't see
your worth because
no one told them of
their own.

dear self,

forgive yourself
for choosing
pain when *peace*
was always an option.

by loving yourself
unconditionally
you are teaching others
how you deserve
to be loved.

dear self,

still in your woundedness
you are worthy.
still in your pain
you are strong.
still in your loneliness
you are loved.

always.

the universe can only
give you what you have
space to hold.

so maybe it's time
to put some stuff down.

dear self,

your body.
your home.

they are the same.

i pray that you embrace
every part of you.

even the parts you
try hard to forget.

dear self,

sit with your joy
the same way
you sit with your
pain.

be gentle with yourself —

you're slowly growing into
the person you've always
wanted to become.

dear self,

your superpower is
that you are still here.
despite everything
you are still

standing strong.

you deserve a love
that you can
heal in.

dear self,

let self-love
be the *root*
to your *rise.*

it's time for you
to be for yourself
what you *begged*
them to be for you.

dear self,

you already know
the answer.

now you have
to decide if
you'll *listen*.

forgive yourself
for choosing
dysfunction...

again.

dear self,

these seeds
will take time
to *bloom*.

appreciate
the process
until they do.

allow yourself to shine
without the desire
to be seen.

dear self,

you belong in
every room
you walk into.

period.

don't shrink.
don't shrink.
don't shrink.
don't shrink.
don't shrink.
don't shrink.

ever.

dear self,

stop trying to find
peace of mind
in people that
never brought you
peace.

you are allowed
to say *no*
without an
explanation.

dear self,

listen to your
emotions.

they come with
many lessons.

you are healing the
generational trauma
your ancestors never
got the chance to.

don't give up.

dear self,

hold space
for yourself
today.

what do you need?

reminder —

you can't love people
out of dysfunction.

dear self,

you have to be
okay with
leaving people
behind.

give it to the moon.
she'll know what
to do with it.

dear self,

you are never alone.
even when your heart
feels the most

lonely.

i can't tell you that this
healing will be easy

but i can assure you
that *it will be worth it.*

dear self,

love shouldn't
feel that way.

let them go.

you are still
seeking perfection.

that's the problem.

dear self,

them not seeing your worth
makes them unworthy —

not you.

you are capable of being
in healthy relationships.

the ones that do not
require you to *fold.*

dear self,

there is nothing wrong
with not always rising.

sometimes it's best to
sit with the pain and
rise once it passes.

you will
always
be enough
for you.

dear self,

choose you —
even when
no one else does.

be patient with yourself.
becoming takes time.

dear self,

if you're tired of
reliving the pain

*try harder to
learn the lesson.*

your heart is tender
from past pain

but it's still worthy
of feeling *strong love.*

dear self,

stop worrying about
what was so you can
receive what was
always *meant to be.*

some friendships
aren't meant to last.

so don't make them.

dear self,

you can put your
savior cape
away for today
and let someone
save you for once.

you survived
the very pain
that you thought
would end you.

i'm so proud of you.

dear self,

forgive them not because
they deserve your forgiveness
but because you deserve
the *freedom* that
will come from it.

it's okay to not know
where to go from here.

maybe this is where
you're meant to
stay for a while.

dear self,

sometimes when
things break
you aren't meant

to *fix them.*

don't expect them to
be for you what you
haven't decided
to *consistently*
be for yourself.

dear self,

let your only regret
be that you didn't
leave sooner.

your season
of hurting is
ending.

dear self,

your season
of healing is
beginning.

your worth is
not based on
your *mistakes*.

dear self,

love doesn't have
to be hard.

love
doesn't
have
to
be
hard.

there won't always
be light to bask in.

sometimes the *darkness*
will be the only place
to reside.

dear self,

find comfort
in knowing
that you made
the right choice.

pull out the weeds
cut the dead flowers
and plant love in the
tender soil of your heart.

dear self,

forgive yourself for going back
when you shouldn't have.
forgive yourself for choosing
them instead of you.
forgive yourself for loving people
who could never love you back.
forgive yourself for thinking pain
was the only thing you were
capable of feeling.

i forgive you.

you deserve the same love
you give out *freely*
to others.

dear self,

you don't have to shrink
to feel seen.
you don't have to shrink
to be heard.
you don't have to shrink
to be loved.
someone will love you
in your *fullness*.

sometimes the most
you can do
is *try*.

dear self,

the only fairytale worth
remembering is the one
that *lives in you.*

how they treat others
is how they will
treat you.

*don't think you
can change them.*

dear self,

it's okay to not be *happy*
with how your story is going.

even if everyone else
says it's going well.

patience tamarra

new beginnings
often feel like
sad endings.

dear self,

if they make you feel like
your love is too much
tell them that it is —

too much for them.

you are allowed
to kiss your wounds
until they *heal*.

dear self,

reminder —

your love will be
too big for some people
to hold.

a flower may
bloom overnight
but the foundation
below the soil
took time to settle in.

be patient.

dear self,

you don't have to
hurt anymore.

don't expect people to
always show up for you

when they're still
figuring out how to
show up for *themselves*.

dear self,

let your faith in love
outweigh any doubts
that *surround* it.

the world *needs you*.
every single part
and piece of you.

dear self,

some people will see
that your cup is full
and *purposely* spill theirs
just to take from yours.

who are you when the door
closes behind you?
when the armor is placed
back on its hanger?
when the drapes are closed?

be that person all the time.

dear self,

when one door closes
find a new way in.

you are alive.

let that be
enough
today.

dear self,

stop pretending
the *red flags*
are green.

you don't have to
accept less than what
you know you deserve
just because it is all
they have to offer.

someone else will
offer you more.

dear self,

someone can hold
your hand through
this struggle

but you have
to *let them.*

if you feel lost
find peace in knowing
that from here
you can only be

found.

dear self,

there is **nothing**
left for you
in the past.

accept all the
changes that life
throws your way.

even when they
feel achingly
uncomfortable.

dear self,

you are love.
you are loved.

you are love.
you are loved.

you are love.
you are loved.

your search
for belonging
in other people
ends today.

*you belong to
no one
but yourself.*

dear self,

stop trying to
fix people

when you're
still *broken*
yourself.

when your bed
starts to cry out
for them again

*don't forget
why you left.*

dear self,

holding onto past pain
is keeping you from
present peace.

let go.

you don't have
to be a
punching bag
for their
insecurities.

dear self,

you are not broken
you just need a little

reshaping.

love is safe.

dear self,

you are beautiful.

if anyone tells you
otherwise remind them
that the same power
lives within them too.

sometimes the
best reply

is **silence.**

dear self,

saying no to things
that don't fill you
is an act of *self-love*

not selfishness.

loving them
from a distance
doesn't mean you
love them any less.

it just means you
love you more.

dear self,

temporary loneliness
will always be better
than *permanent* scars.

maybe the miracle
you've been praying for
has been praying for you.

you're the miracle.

dear self,

today is a *blank canvas*.

choose to paint
it with bright
and vibrant colors.

not everyone is
out to hurt you.

it's safe to let
some people in.

dear self,

be open to your dream
not looking the way
you want it to

because it could be
closer than you think.

reminder —

healing requires
patience.

dear self,

you still shine bright
even when no one is
there to *witness*
your light.

you are **not** responsible
for anyone's healing
but your own.

dear self,

stop
procrastinating
on your *dreams*.

access to your energy
is a *privilege*
not all are
worthy of receiving.

dear self,

grow flowers
in the empty spaces
they planted in
your heart.

be the person
your younger self
needed growing up

because they
still do.

dear self,

you can't yet see
the light at the end
of the tunnel
because the light
is in *you*.

you can't
stand in *faith*
and worry
at the same time.

dear self,

don't pretend like
you didn't cause
them pain too.

you're not the only
victim in this story.

*be gentle
with yourself.*

you are doing
your best.

dear self,

what happens next
is out of your hands.

what happens now
is all up to you.

reminder —

you should never feel
the need to perform
around people that
claim they love you.

dear self,

your standards
aren't high.

they just can't
reach them.

you'll continue going
through these trials
until you learn the lesson.

take notes this time around.

dear self,

you can choose
to rise, or not.

either way
your choice
is *valid*.

patience is your way
of showing the universe
you believe in its magic.

dear self,

remember you did
the best you could
with what you had.

even when you
didn't have much.

that which you require
from others you must
first require from
yourself.

dear self,

whatever you do
never stop
loving hard.

it isn't your
job to fix
them.

family included.

dear self,

tell them how you feel
even if they don't listen.
someone will hear you.

even if that someone
is just you.

don't let them make
you an option
when you deserve
to be a *priority.*

dear self,

build tapestries
out of your pain
so you can see
that *beauty* still
exist in you.

reminder —

you can always
start again.

thank you for growing with me.

patience tamarra
@patiencetamarra

dear self,

Author: Patience Tamarra